The flavour of the Canaries
on your table

Juan Carlos Suárez Felipe
Jesús Diógenes Álvarez Toledo

Translation by
Shubhaa Villanueva Roca

1st edition 2002
Depósito legal: G.C. 623 - 2002
ISBN: 84 - 932901 - 1 - 4
Printed in Las Palmas de Gran Canaria
Editado por J. & J. EDICIONES GRÁFICAS, S.L.
TLS: 620 999 340 / 620 999 341

Acknowledgements

We would like to show our gratitude to:

Mª de Pino Inglott Domínguez, Doña Constanza, Mrs Maruca, Auntie Carmen, Pilar Reyes Cáceres, Doña María, Mrs Pino, Ángeles Salom Martín, Carmen Castillo de Paz, and of course, to the Chef in charge of "Monumento al Campesino", Mr. Servando Martín Pérez and his team of waiters and cooks for their colaboration and service when elaborating these dishes.

Without the help of all these friends of the Canarian cooking we would have never been able to bring this work to reality.

The flavour of the
Canaries
on your table
·5·

The flavour of the Canaries
on your table

With such a title it would be just great to take advantadge of it and get in the kitchen, get the utensiles, put the apron on and prepare the ingredients to start enjoying Canarian cooking, The feeling of these dishes, based upon recipes given by people from our land, will leave you with a memory of the Canaries on your palate.

With this recipe book-guide we just want to bring the Canarian flavour to your table in an easy and practical way, so that you can enjoy these meals at home.

We have tried to explain those ingredients which cannot be translated into English, as well as the utensiles and cooking techniques. We have also add a small dictionary of traditional Canarian cooking terminology.

And that said, let's work and bon appetit!

The flavour of the
Canaries
on your table
·7·

Ball of Gofio

Preparation: 8 minutes

What we need:
· 250 gr corn gofio[1]
· 1 dessert spoon of olive oil
· 1 teaspoon of sugar
· 1 glass of water
· 1 pinch of salt

How to do it:
1. Put the gofio in a bowl, add the oil, sugar, water and salt. Knead very well (better with your hands than with a spoon)
2. When you have formed a ball, cut it like bread and serve on a large serving dish for people to serve themselves.
3. The ball of gofio goes well with mojo, cheese, olives, fish, broth, meat, and of course a good wine.

---

[1] Gofio, the historical meal of the Canarian gastronomie, consists of flour (wheat or corn) and can be combined with everything. It can be kneaded with meat, fish, broth, desserts...we Canarian people say that gofio is our bread

The flavour of the
Canaries
on your table
.9.

Red "Mojo" Sauce

Preparation: 15 minutes plus one and a half days to settle.

What we need:
- 8-9 cloves of garlic
- 1 red dry pepper from La Palma (you can use cayenne pepper instead)
- 1 small handfull of cumin seeds
- 1 dessert spoon of thick cooking salt
- 1 dessert spoon of red sweet paprika
- 1 small glass of wine vinegar
- 1 glass of olive oil
- 10 minced roasted almonds
- 1 glass of water

How to do it:
1. Boil the water with the cayenne pepper for about 10 seconds. Leave it to settle for 2 hours.
2. Press dry the pepper and dry with paper serviettes. Keep the water to one side and mix the pepper with the garlic, cumin seeds, salt, sweet paprika, vinegar, oil and almonds. When mixed, leave to settle in the fridge for one and a half days.
3. On day 2 take the mixture and make a puré with a food blender.
4. Add the water you used to boil the cayenne to the previously obtained puré and the mojo[2] is ready to be served with potatoes, fish, cheese...

---

[2] This sauce can be kept in the fridge a few weeks by adding a bit of extra olive oil and keeping it in a closed jar. Leave it in the lower part of the fridge (less cold)

The flavour of the
Canaries
on your table
·11·

Green "Mojo" Sauce

Preparation: 10 minutes plus settling

What we need:
- 6 cloves of garlic
- 1/2 glass of olive oil
- 1/2 green hot pepper
- 1 dribble of vinegar
- 1 handfull of parsley or coriander
- 1 small glass of water
- 1 dessert spoon of thick salt

How to do it
1. Wash the coriander or parsley and chop with the garlic. Mash in the mortar with the salt and pepper.
2. When you have made it into a puré, add the oil and vinegar. If you want it thinner, add a bit of water.

This mojo goes with all sorts of fish and shellfish, and of course, with Canarian potatoes[3].

---

[3] Same conservation than the previous mojo rojo (see recipe)

The flavour of the
Canaries
on your table
·12·

Mojo Sauce with Cheese

Preparation: 8 minutes.

What we need:
· A piece of white hard cheese.
· 6 cloves of garlic
· 1 red pepper
· 1 small glass of olive oil
· Salt

Note: the only secret of the mojo sauce is to beat it very very well.

How to do it:
1. Wash the pepper, remove the seeds and chop it. Chop the cheese in small pieces. Add the skinned garlic, the salt and half the glass of oil. Beat in the mixer.
2. Beat the mixture very well, add the rest of the oil and keep on beating. After a minute, add a small glass of water, beat a bit more and ready.

The flavour of the
Canaries
on your table
·13·

Reddish Mojo Sauce for roast (Reddish)

Preparation: 10 minutes

What we need:
· Bread crumbs
· 4 cloves of garlic
· 1 small glass of olive oil
· 3 dessert spoons of vinegar
· 1 pinch of thick salt
· 1 pinch of saffron
· 1 teaspoon of cayenne pepper
· 1 teaspoon of cumin

How to do it:
1. Heat the saffron in a frying pan. When it is heated, put it in the morter and mash with the bread crumbs, which we had previously soacked in a bit of oil. Add the chopped garlic and mash well. Add the salt, cumin, cayenne pepper and finally the rest of the oil with the vinegar. Mash again and ready.

The flavour of the
Canaries
on your table
·14·

Mojo Sauce from La Palma Island

Preparation: 15 minutes.

What we need:
· 6 red dry peppers
· 1 bulb of garlic
· 1 teaspoon of cumin
· 1 teaspoon of oregano
· 4 black pepper grains
· 1 small handful of thick cooking salt
· 1 small glass of vinegar
· 1 teaspoon of paprika
· 1/2 litre oil
· 100 gr minced roasted almonds

How to do it:
1. Put the dry peppers with a bit of water in a small saucepan and leave settle for 3-4 hours.
2. Peel the cloves of garlic, cut in half, add cumin, oregano, black pepper, paprika, the almonds, the vinegar and a bit of oil. Remove the seeds from the peppers, add a bit of the water we had left them in and mix in the mixer.
3. Add the thick cooking salt and the rest of the oil. Mix for 2 more minutes.

This mojo sauce can be kept for two years in a vacuum-packed glass jar.

Recipe by courtesy of Mrs. Maruca

The flavour of the
Canaries
on your table
·15·

Mild Mojo Sauce from Pino Santo

Preparation: 1/2 hour

What we need:
· 1 Kg ripe tomatoes
· 1/2 glass of oil
· 6 teaspoons of vinegar
· 3-4 small packets of cumin seeds
· Salt
· Water
· Chopped parsley
· Coriander

How to do it:
1. Boil the tomatoes, remove the skin while hot. Remove the seeds and mix with the oil.
2. Mash the parsley and the chopped coriander with the salt.
3. Beat all by hand or with the mixer and add a bit of water if it is too thick (some people add 1/2 glass vegetable broth with the salt)

Recipe by Mrs. Pine, from Pino Santo, by courtesy of
Ángeles Salom Martín.

The flavour of the
Canaries
on your table
·16·

Canarian Potatoes

Preparation: 45 minutes

What we need:
· 1 Kg small or medium potatoes
· 100 gr thick cooking salt
· 1 thick slice of lemon

How to do it:
1. Wash the potatoes very well. If necessary use a cloth to remove sand or dirt.
2. Put the potatoes in a cooking pot and add water to just cover them. Add the lemon and the salt and cook on a high flame.
3. When the potatoes are cooked, prick with a fork. If the fork goes through easily, the potatoes are ready.
4. Drain the water and then leave the pot on the flame till the rest of the water evaporates.

The flavour of the
Canaries
on your table
·17·

Canarian Sancocho

(Typical Canarian fish dish)

Preparation : 30 minutes

What we need:
· 1 Kg salted cherne (typical Canarian fish)[4]
· 1/2 Kg yellow sweet potatoes
· 1 Kg potatoes
· 1 onion
· Salt and vinegar
· Ball of gofio (see recipe)
· Red mojo (see recipe)

How to do it:
1. Leave the salted cherne in water for a day, changing the water 2-3 times. It must be kept in a fresh place or in the fridge.
2. After the fish has been in the water for a day, chop the potaotes and the sweet potatoes into big pieces. Place the fish, the potatoes and the sweet potatoes in a pan. Add water and cook on a high flame 20-25 minutes. Drain the water and let settle for a few minutes with the lid half open for the steam to get out.
3. Meanwhile chop the onion in rings and place on a plate with a bit of salt and vinegar. Leave to be served with the fish.
4. Place the fish, potatoes and sweet potatoes on a large serving dish.
5. Serve with the ball of gofio, the onion in sauce and the red mojo.
6. It goes well with a salad of lettuce, tomatoe, cucumber and pepper with light dressing.

Recipe by courtesy of Dᵃ Constanza (Tenerife)

---

[4] Cherne is a typical dry salted fish.

The flavour of the
Canaries
on your table
·19·

Vieja in Sauce

(Vieja = typical Canarian fish)

Preparation: 20 minutes for the fish
10 minutes for the sauce

What we need for the special sauce:
· Pepper · Parsley
· Cumin · Garlic
· Olive oil · Wine vinegar
· 1 pepper · Salt

How to do it:
1. Mix the garlic, cumin, finely chopped parsley, pepper and a piece of the pepper. Mash it all until it becomes a fine paste. Add the vinegar, oil and mix well. The sauce is ready.

What we need for the vieja fish:
· 1 tomato
· 1 onion
· 1 leaf of bay
· Olive oil
· 1 teaspoon of vinegar

How to do it:
1. Fill a pan with water, add the tomato, the onion chopped in four pieces, the bay, oil and vinegar.
2. Heat it all and when the water starts boiling put the vieja fish in and reduce the flame. Cook for 12 minutes.
3. Take the fish from the pot, remove the skin, the scales and the side bones.
4. Serve in a large serving dish with Canarian potatoes and, of course, the special sauce.

Recipe by courtesy of Dᵃ Enriqueta (La Graciosa)

Soused Fish

Preparation: 1 hour

What we need:
- 1 Kg of fish in slices
- 5 medium onions
- 1 bulb of garlic
- Oil to fry
- Bay
- Thyme
- 1 small glass of vinegar
- Sweet paprika
- 1 pinch of salt
- 1 bread roll
- Water

How to do it:
1. Fry the floured fish. Cut the onion in rings and fry in the same oil. Place it all in a china bowl.
2. Cut the bread and the garlic in slices. Fry in the same oil as the fish and mash in the morter.
3. Put the remaining paste in the frying pan with the paprika, bay, thyme, salt, vinegar and a small glass of water. Heat for 5 minutes stirring with a wooden spoon.
4. When the sauce is ready, pour onto the fish and onion and serve with boiled or Canarian potatoes.

Recipe by courtesy of Mª del Pino Inglott Domínguez (Mapi)

The flavour of the
Canaries
on your table
·21·

Young Goat "Embarrao"
(in Sauce)

Preparation: 2 hours

What we need:
2.5 Kg young goat meat in medium size pieces

For the "embarrao" sauce:
· 6 teaspoons of sweet paprika
· 1 teaspoon of hot paprika
· 7 mashed cloves of garlic
· 1 small handfull of fresh or dry thyme
· 1 small glass o wine vinegar
· 1 bottle white wine (not in carton)
· 6 teaspoons red mojo (see recipe 3)
· Salt

The "embarrao" sauce is a fine mixure of all these ingredients.

How to do it:
1. Put the washed pieces of goat in a big bowl with the "embarrao" sauce and leave for 24 hours.
2. Take the pieces of meat and dry with paper serviettes. Fry in olive oil with 2-3 cloves of garlic (with skin). When the meat is well-fried, lay on a serving dish with a lid on top.
3. Put the oil you just used to fry the meat in with the remaining "embarrao" sauce in a pan. Cook on a low flame for 5 minutes and on a high flame 5 more minutes until the sauce thickens.
4. Put the meat in the pan and mix well. Leave to settle for 2 hours.
5. After 2 hours, heat on a medium flame for 25 minutes and settle for 10 minutes before serving.

The flavour of the
Canaries
on your table
·22·

6. While the meat is settling, boil potatoes to serve with it.

Recipe by courtesy of Jesús Diógenes Álvarez Toledo

Rabbit in "Salmorejo" Sauce

Preparation: aprox. 1 hour

What we need:
· 2 Kg of rabbit
· 1/2 litre olive oil

For the sauce:
· 6 cloves of garlic
· 1 dessert spoon of thick cooking salt
· 1 red cayenne pepper
· 1 dessert spoon of sweet paprika
· 2-3 small thyme branches
· 1 pinch of oregano
· 1/2 litre white wine
· 1 small glass of vinegar
· 1 small glass of olive oil

How to do it:
1. Mash the garlic with the pepper and the thick salt. When it is all well mashed, add the paprika, the vinegar, the white wine and the oil.
2. Place the chopped rabbit on a large serving dish, add the oregano and the thyme, cover with a wet tea towel and leave settle for a while.
3. Drain the meat and fry until it browns a bit.
4. Place the meat in an earthenware pot. Put the sauce in a pan and reduce a bit.
5. Mix the sauce with the meat and cook on low flame for 10 minutes.
6. If it is too dry, add a bit of white wine.
7. This dish can be served with Canarian or cooked potatoes.

Recipe by courtesy of Dª Constanza

The flavour of the
Canaries
on your table
·25·

Chickpeas Soup

Preparation: 1 hour

What we need:
· 1/2 Kg chickpeas
· 2 medium onions
· 1 bit of bacon
· 1 bit of black pudding
· 1 bit of hard pork sausage
· Garlic
· 1 small glass of white wine
· 1 bay leaf
· 1 bit of fried tomato

How to do it:
1. Cook the chickpeas with the pork sausage, the black pudding and the bacon.
2. While the chickpeas are cooking, prepare a sauce frying the onions with the garlic and the fried tomato.
3. When the chickpeas are cooked, add the sauce and boil again with the white wine, the bay leaf and some salt.
4. When it starts boiling again, it is ready.

Watch out!
The chickpeas must be left in water the night before to soften.

Recipe by courtesy of Carmen Castillo de Paz (La Palma island)

The flavour of the
Canaries
on your table
·27·

Ropa Vieja

("Old Clothes": typical Canarian stew)

Preparation: 1 hour

What we need:
· 1/2 Kg chickpeas
· 3/4 Kg meat
· 2-3 medium size carrots
· 1 big onion
· 1/2 bulb of garlic
· Parsley
· 3 eggs
· 1 Kg potatoes in dices

How to do it:
1. Cook the meat with the chickpeas, the carrot and the onion.
2. Fry each ingredient separately.
3. Fry the potatoes.
4. Mix all the ingredients again in a high pan (more comfortable)
5. Mash the garlic with the parsley and a pinch of salt.
6. Add the resulting mixture in the pan.
7. Add the eggs (without beating them) and stirr on low flame until the egg is cooked.

Watch out!
The chickpeas must be left in water the night before to soften.
You can use the remaining broth to make soup.

Recipe by courtesy of Carmen Castilla de Paz (La Palma island)

The flavour of the
Canaries
on your table
·28·

Rosco
(Canarian doughnuts)

Preparation: 1 hour more or less

What we need:
· 3 eggs
· 3 glasses of oil
· 3 glasses of sugar
· Grated lemon skin
· 1 teaspoon of baking powder
· 1/2 Kg baking flour
· 1 teaspoon of cinnamon powder
· Oil to fry

How to do it:
1. Mix all the ingredients and beat very well.
2. Add the flour while mixing to make a fine dough.
3. Shape the doughnuts and fry in very hot oil.

Recipe by courtesy of Auntie Carmen

The flavour of the
Canaries
on your table
·29·

Mole Eggs

Preparation: 1 hour

What we need:
· 12 egg yolks
· 12 spoons of sugar
· Water

How to do it
1. Put the sugar in a pan and cover with water. Heat it until it becomes a thick syrup. Remove from the heat and let settle.
2. Beat the egg yolks until creamy (by hand or with a mixer). Add the syrup and beat for a few secs to mix well.
3. Place the pot in boiling water (baine Marie) until it thickens. When the thickened mixture loosens from the pan sides, the dessert is ready.
4. Serve in cups or bowls and let cool.
5. Serve with a teaspoon of gofio

Recipe by courtesy of Mª del Pino Inglott Domínguez (Mapi)

The flavour of the
Canaries
on your table
·31·

Torrija

Preparation: more or less 1/2 hour

What we need:
· 1/2 litre milk
· 1/4 litre white wine
· 2 eggs
· 1 teaspoon of cinnamon powder
· 1 dessert spoon of grated lemon skin
· 100 gr sugar
· 1 teaspoon of baking powder
· 1/2 kg baking flour
· Oil to fry
· Icing sugar

How to do it:
1. Beat the eggs. Add the milk (room temperature), the wine, the sugar, the lemon skin, the baking powder, the cinnamon and the sugar.
2. Mix well and add the flour while mixing to make a fine dough.
3. Put dessert spoons of the mixture in hot oil to obtain the "torrijas"
4. Once fried, drain the oil and sprinkle with the icing sugar

Recipe by courtesy of Auntie Carmen

The flavour of the
Canaries
on your table
·33·

Cream Caramel

What we need:
· 370 gr condensed milk
· 1 glass of milk
· 6 eggs
· 1 lemon
· Sugar

How to do it:
1. Separate the egg whites from the yolks. Whip the egg whites.
2. Mix the yolks with the milk, the grated lemon skin and the condensed milk.
3. When it is all well mixed, add the whipped egg whites stirring slowly.
4. Heat the sugar on low flame with a drop of lemon juice. Mix until it becomes a syrup.
5. Pour the syrup in the mould and add the mixture.
6. Place the mould in boiling water (baine Marie) in the oven for 45 minutes at 180°.
7. Remove from its mould when it is cold.
8. This cream caramel can be kept in the fridge for 48 hours.

Recipe by courtesy of Doña María

The flavour of the
Canaries
on your table
·35·

Bread Sweet

Preparation: 30 minutes.

What we need:
· 6 hard bread rolls
· 6 eggs
· 1 grated lemon skin
· 1 teaspoon of cinnamon powder
· 1 small packet of anise seeds
· 1 tin of condensed milk
· 1 litre milk (to soak the bread)
· 2 dessert spoons of butter

How to do it:
The previous night leave the bread to soak with the milk, the cinnamon, the anise and the lemon skin.

1. Put the previous mixture in the mixer and beat. Add the sugar, the condensed milk, the eggs, the butter and mix well.
2. Grease a mould. Pour the mixture in the mould and bake for 45 minutes at 160°. To check if it is ready, prick with a toothpick. If it comes out clean, it is ready.
3. Leave settle until it cools down to room temperature.

Recipe by courtesy of Pilar Reyes Cáceres

The flavour of the
Canaries
on your table
·36·

Dictionary of traditional Canarian cooking terminology

CANARIAN SPANISH	ENGLISH
Caldero:	*Cooking pot*
Gofio:	*Toasted flour*
Hondilla:	*Bowl*
Lebrillo:	*Serving dish*
Matalahúga/matalahúva:	*Anise seeds*
Millo:	*Corn*
Papas:	*Potatoes*
Pella:	*Ball of dough*
Sancochar:	*Cook, boil*

· *PELLA DE GOFIO (BALL OF GOFIO)*
· *MOJO ROJO (RED "MOJO" SAUCE)*
· *MOJO VERDE (GREEN "MOJO" SAUCE)*
· *MOJO SAUCE WITH CHEESE*
· *MILD MOJO SAUCE FROM PINO SANTO*
· *PAPAS ARRUGADAS*
· *CANARIAN SANCOCHO*
· *VIEJA IN SAUCE*
· *SOUSED FISH*
· *YOUNG GOAT "EMBARRAO"*
· *RABBIT IN "SALMOREJO"*
· *"ROPA VIEJA"*
· *CHICKPEAS SOUP*
· *MOLE EGGS*
· *TORRIJA*
· *ROSCO (CANARIAN DOUGHNUTS)*
· *BREAD SWEET*
· *CREAM CARAMEL*

The flavour of the
Canaries
on your table
·37·